INSPiRoLOGY

This quirky colouring book is waiting to inspire you. Find an inspirational quote then colour the beautiful lettering and intricate pictures. Create your own stunning quote designs by tracing the letters and pictures at the back of this book on to blank paper.

SUCCESS

Believing in yourself is the key to success in all areas of life. These quotes are all about hard work, self-belief and achieving your dreams.

PEOPLE
RARELY SUCCEED
unless they
HAVE
FUN
IN WHAT THEY ARE DOING.

the People who
enough to think
to think
the World
are the

are CRAZY
they can CHANGE
ONES that DO
Steve Jobs

A Problem is a chance for you to do your best
Duke Ellington

If you aren't in over your head, how do you know how tall you are?
~ T.S. Eliot

SHOOT FOR
EVEN IF YOU
FAIL AMONG
Les

THE MOON
MESS
THE
YOU'L
STARS
Broken

Life is like Riding a Bicycle to keep your Balance

you must keep moving
albert Einstein

DON'T
LOOK BACK
YOU'RE
NOT
GOING
THAT
WAY.

IF at first you DO SUCCEED, try to hide your ASTONISHMENT
HARRY F. BANKS

ALL
OUR DREAMS CA
IF WE HAVE THE
TO PURSU

COME TRUE,
COURAGE
THEM. ~ Walt Disney

HARD TIMES

The tough times make us appreciate the good times. These quotes are here to remind you that things will get better.

STARS
CAN'T
SHINE
WITHOUT
DARKNESS

IF WE HAD NO WINTER

the Spring would not be so pleasant
Anne Bradstreet

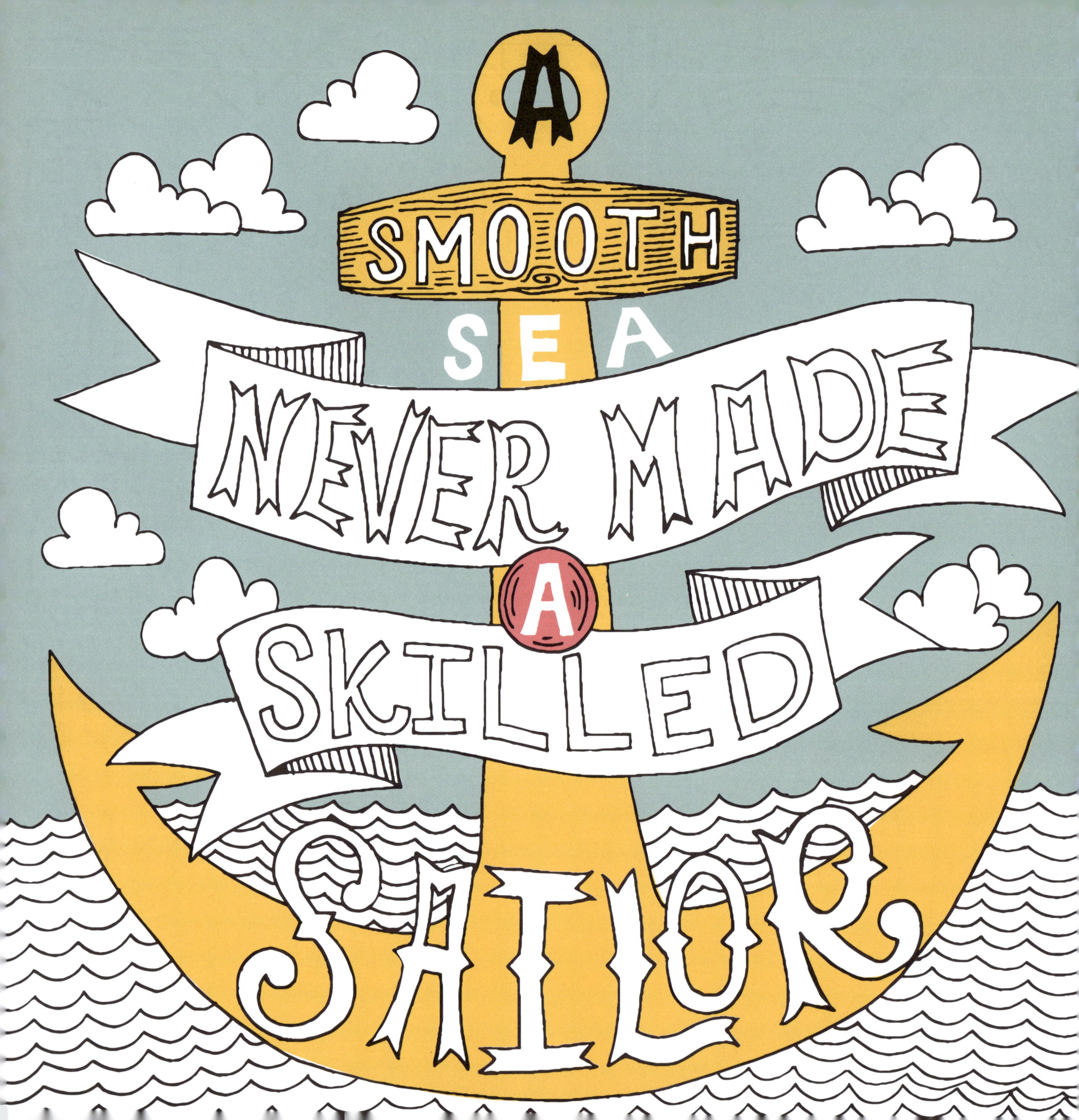

SMOOTH SEA
NEVER MADE
A
SKILLED
SAILOR

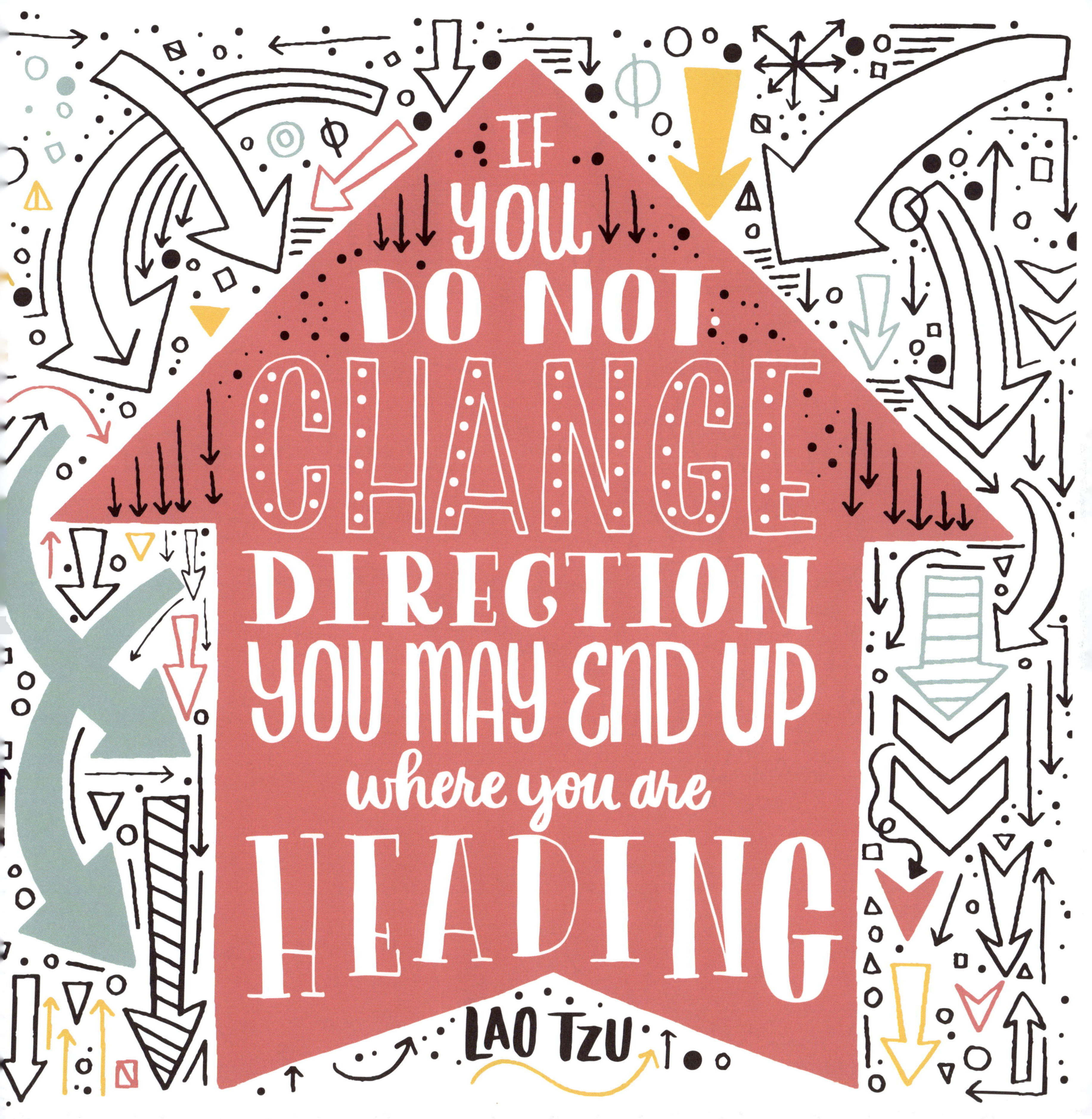

IF YOU DO NOT CHANGE DIRECTION YOU MAY END UP where you are HEADING
LAO TZU

DON'T BE
Discouraged
It's often

the
Key
the
in the
bunch
LAST
that
OPENS
the
lock

Don't cry because it's
over, smile because it
happened

WHEN it RAINS
look FOR RAINBOWS
WHEN IT'S DARK
look FOR STARS

THE DIFFERENCE BETWEEN stumbling BLOCKS

& stepping stones
is how you use them

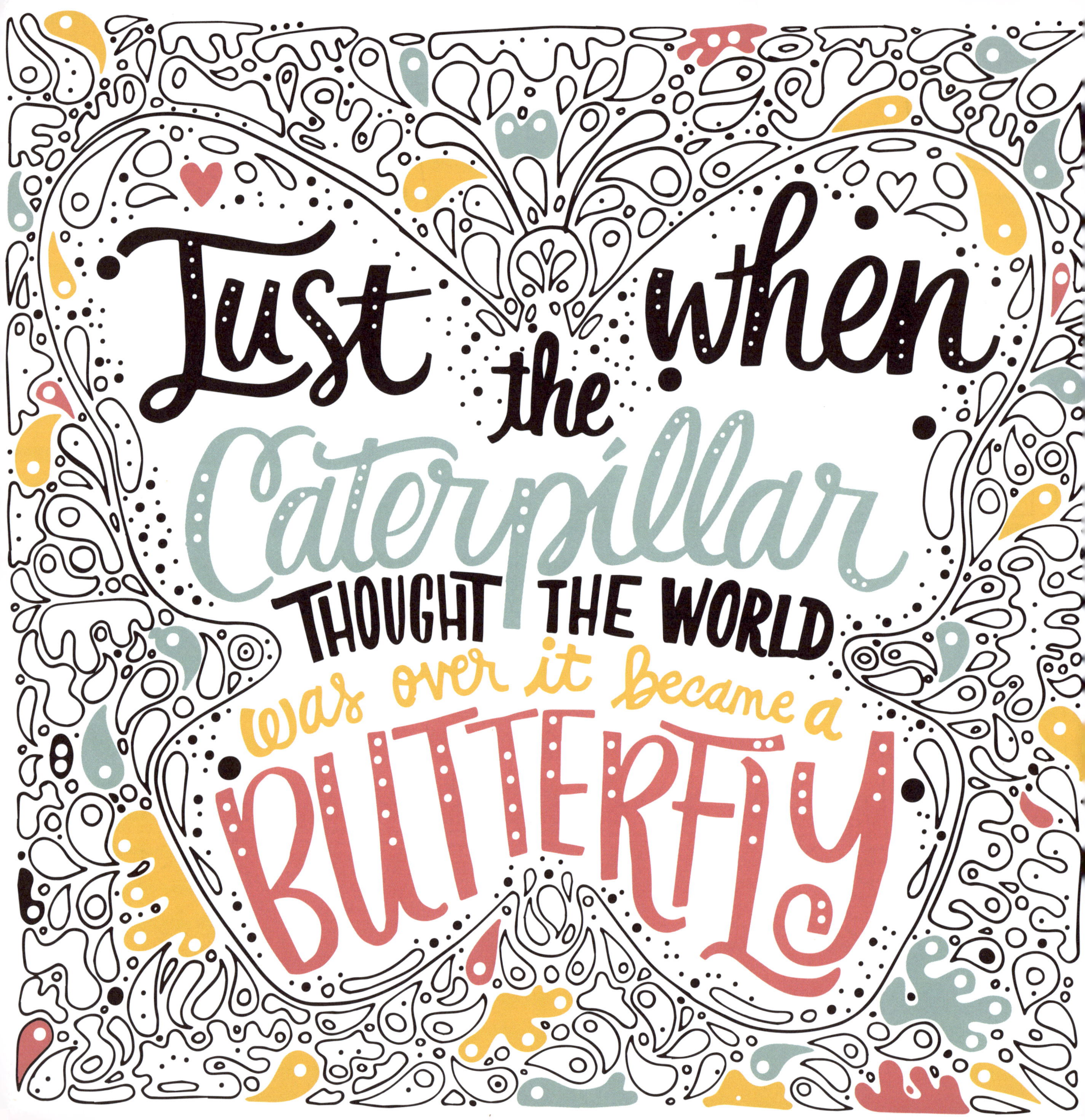

Just
the
when
Caterpillar
THOUGHT THE WORLD
was over it became a
BUTTERFLY

Life IS like
PHOTOGRAPHY.
YOU NEED THE NEGATIVES
to DEVELOP.

POSITIVE THOUGHTS

Having a positive outlook on life can help you on the road to happiness. These quotes are about kindness, joy and being true to yourself.

THE BEST
DREAMS
HAPPEN
WHEN YOU'RE
AWAKE

COUNT YOUR JOYS INSTEAD OF YOUR WOES

COUNT YOUR
FRIENDS
INSTEAD OF
YOUR FOES

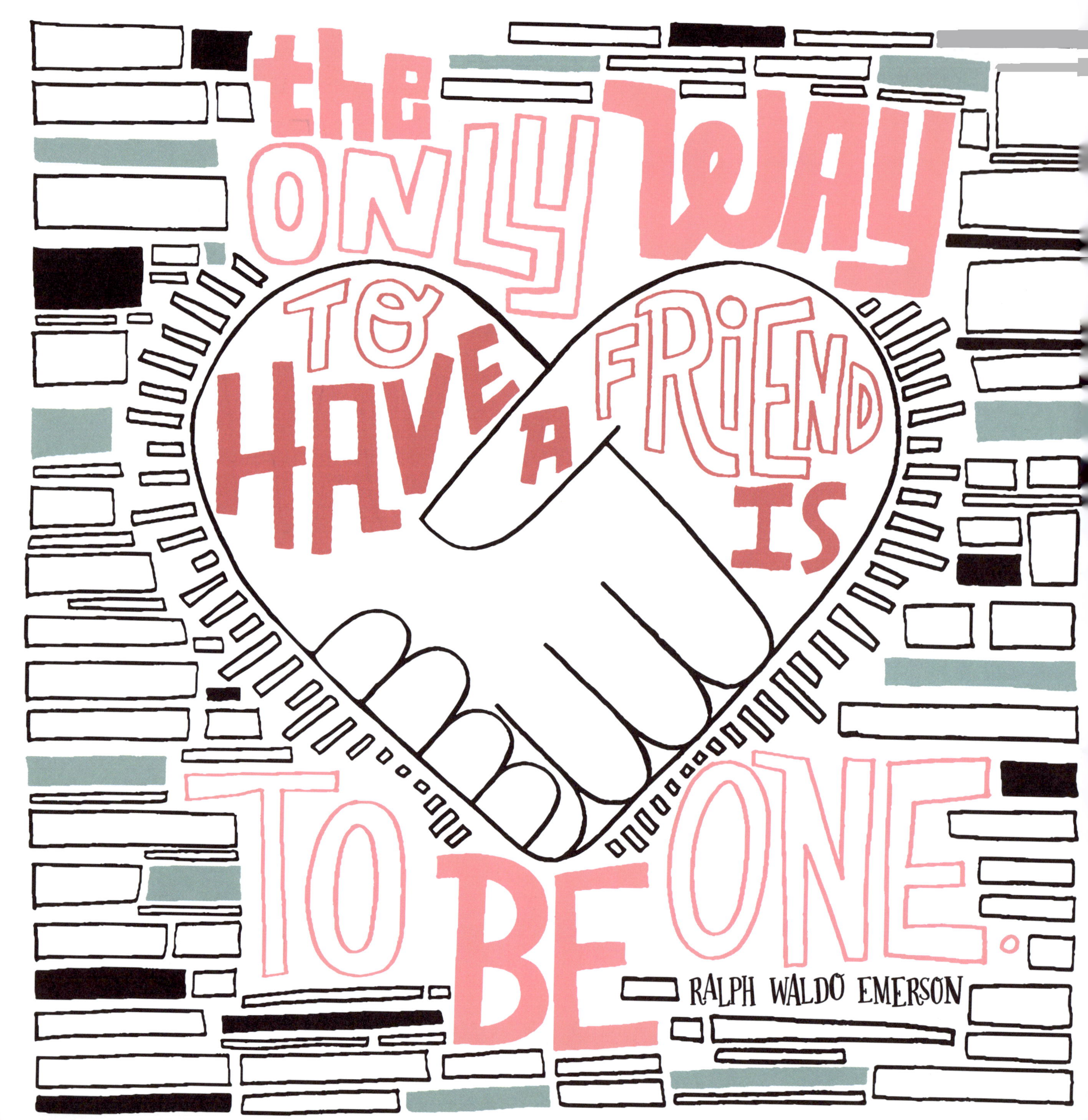

the only way
to have a friend is
to be one.
RALPH WALDO EMERSON

BE YOURSELF; EVERYONE ELSE IS ALREADY TAKEN.

Oscar Wilde

TURN YOUR
FACE
to the
SUN

& THE SHADOWS FALL BEHIND YOU.

The grass is greener where you water it
~ Neil Barringham

Life
DOES
NOT
HAVE TO BE
PERFECT
TO BE
WONDERFUL
ANNETTE FUNICELLO

HAPPINESS OFTEN SNEAKS IN THROUGH A DOOR

YOU DIDN'T KNOW YOU LEFT OPEN
~ JOHN BARRYMORE

LIFE ISN'T ABOUT FINDING YOURSELF

LIFE IS
ABOUT
CREATING
YOURSELF

TRAVEL & ADVENTURE

Whether you are going on a metaphorical
or an actual journey, these quotes will help
you find your path. Embrace adventure
and see what happens!

WHEREVER YOU GO, GO
with ALL your of HEART.
Confucius

PEOPLE
DON'T TAKE TRIPS
TRIPS
TAKE
PEOPLE

if you come to a FORK in the ROAD, take it.
THIS
THAT
Yogi Berra

DO NOT FOLLOW
WHERE the
PATH may LEAD.

"Go instead where there is no path & leave a trail."

Ralph Waldo Emerson

TAKE ONLY MEMORIES,
LEAVE ONLY FOOTPRINTS
CHIEF SEATTLE

The Journey of 1000 Miles begins with a Single Step
Lao Tzu

You can never cross
the OCEAN
UNTIL
YOU HAVE THE

COURAGE
to
LOSE
SIGHT
of the
SHORE.
~CHRISTOPHER COLUMBUS

NORMALITY
IS A PAVED
ROAD

IT'S Comfortable TO WALK, BUT NO FLOWERS
GROW ON IT.
Vincent van Gogh

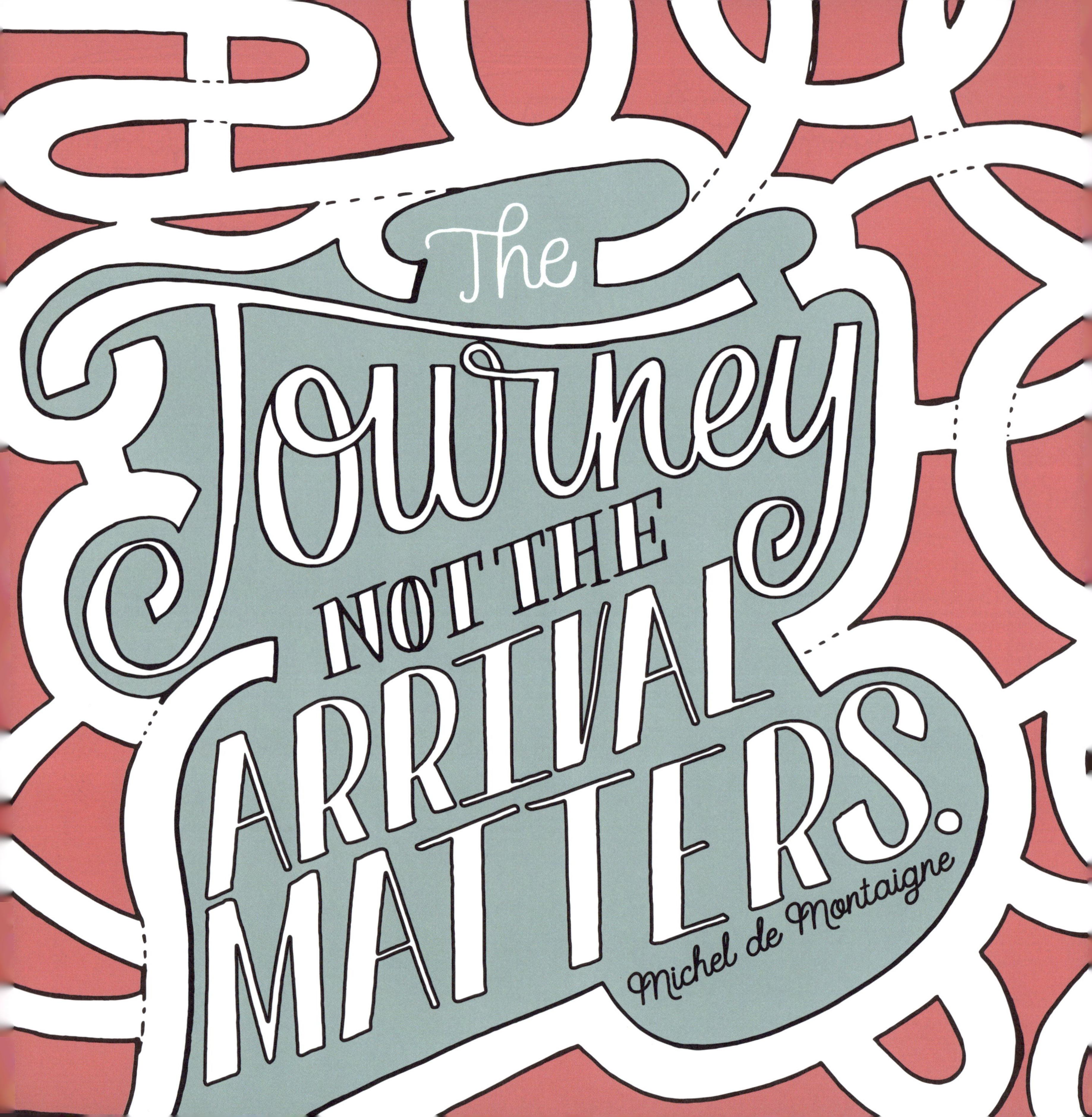

The
Journey
not the
Arrival
Matters.
Michel de Montaigne

A GOOD TRAVELLER HAS NO FIXED PLANS & IS NOT INTENT ON ARRIVING
LAO TZU

TRACE YOUR OWN!
Trace the letters and images on the next few pages on to blank paper and create your own inspiring quotes.
ABCDEFGHIJKLMN
OPQRSTUVWXYZ
abcdefghijklm
nopqrstuvwxyz

ABCDEFG
HIJKLMN
OPQRSTU
VWXYZ?!

a b c d e f g
h i j k l m n
o p q r s t u
v w x y z

A B C D E F G
H I J K L M N
O P Q R S T U
V W X Y Z ! ?

ABCDEFG
HIJKLMN
OPQRSTU
VWXYZ12
34567890

abcdefg
hijklmn
opqrstu
vwxyz?!
1234567890